GW01605516

THE SOURCES OF THE STORIES

There are many versions of the fairy-tales told in this book. The story-tellers listed below wrote, or wrote down, the best-known versions, on which the present tellings are based. The date is the original year of publication.

Jack and the Beanstalk · Joseph Jacobs 1890
The Little Red Hen · Sara Cone Bryant 1907
The Elves and the Shoemaker · Jacob and Wilhelm Grimm 1812
The Princess and the Pea · Hans Christian Andersen 1835

Published exclusively for
J Sainsbury plc
Stamford Street London SE1 9LL
by Walker Books Ltd
184-192 Drummond Street
London NW1 3HP

First published 1985

Printed in Italy.

ISBN 0-7445-0277-2

JACK AND THE BEANSTALK

THE LITTLE RED HEN

THE ELVES AND THE SHOEMAKER

THE PRINCESS AND THE PEA

Retold by Sarah Hayes

Illustrated by Gerrard McIvor

SAINSBURY'S · WALKER BOOKS

JACK AND THE BEANSTALK

There was once a poor widow who lived with her only son Jack, a good-natured but lazy boy. Sometimes he weeded the garden and milked the cow, and sometimes he didn't. But one dry summer the grass turned brown and the cow gave no milk.

'We have no money and no food,' said Jack's mother. 'You will have to take the cow to market and sell her.' Jack was fond of the cow, and he set off to market with a heavy heart.

On the road he met an old man wrapped in a cloak and walking with a stick. 'And where might you be going?' asked the old man, eyeing Jack and the cow. Jack explained his errand, and the old man smiled.

'I might be able to help you,' he said.

'Would you take these in return for your cow?' He held out his hand and showed Jack six shiny coloured beans.

'I want money for my cow, not beans!' said Jack indignantly.

'Ah, but these are no ordinary beans,' replied the old man. 'These are magic beans.'

Jack saw the sun sparkle on the beans in the old man's hand. He thought of the long journey to market, and he made up his mind. 'Agreed,' said Jack, and he took the beans and gave the cow to the old man.

Jack's mother was waiting for him when he arrived home. 'You have been quick,' she said. 'How much did you get for the cow? Where is our money?' Jack held out his hand. His mother looked at the beans in disbelief.

'I got beans instead, Mother,' said Jack. 'Magic beans.'

'Magic beans indeed!' shouted Jack's mother. 'These beans aren't magic, you stupid, lazy, good-for-nothing boy!' In a fury she snatched up the beans, hurled them out of the window and sent Jack to bed without any supper.

When Jack woke the next morning, his bedroom was filled with green light. He rushed to look out of the window and saw that during the night the beans had grown into a giant beanstalk. It curled its way up past Jack's bedroom window, past the roof of the house and up into the clouds.

Now Jack may have been lazy and a little foolish, but he wasn't short of courage. So he climbed straight out of his window and up, up, up to the very top of the beanstalk.

He found himself in a desert land, with no grass, trees or birds. There were only rocks and bare earth, and something that looked like a house in the far distance.

Jack started to walk towards the house, which seemed to grow bigger and bigger, until he found himself at the foot of an enormous door. He knocked and a tall, kind-looking woman opened the door.

'Good morning, Ma'am,' said Jack, who now remembered he had eaten no breakfast or supper. 'Could you spare me a crust of bread?'

'You'll have to be quick,' the woman replied. 'My husband will be home any minute. But I'll see what I can find.'

Jack followed her into the largest room he had ever seen. Two huge chairs stood beside a table so tall that Jack could not see over it.

The woman set Jack on a footstool as big as a double bed and gave him a crust that was twice the size of an ordinary loaf.

While Jack was eating, the floor-boards began to shudder. Pans rattled on the shelves, and the house shook to its foundations.

'Alas, alas, there is my husband come home!' the woman said to Jack. 'Hide in the oven or he will have you for tea.' Jack hopped into the oven, but left the door open a crack.

Loud footsteps stamped up to the door and a great voice bellowed:

'Fee fi fo fum,
I smell the blood of an Englishman.
Be he alive or be he dead,
I'll grind his bones to make my bread.'

'It's only the sheep you killed for your supper,' said the woman.

Jack peeped out of the oven and saw towering above him a huge giant with a spiked club made from a tree trunk. The giant grunted and sat down to eat. He ate and ate until he leant back in his chair and called for his bags of gold. Jack heard the 'chink, chink' of the gold pieces as the giant counted them. Then the chinks slowed down and finally stopped, and the kitchen began to echo with snores. The giant was asleep.

As quietly as possible, Jack climbed out of the oven. He took a bag of gold, tip-toed out of the great house, ran across the desert lands and climbed down the beanstalk and in through his bedroom window.

Jack's mother was delighted with the bag of gold, and for many months she and Jack lived in luxury. But the day came when the bag was empty, and Jack decided to climb the magic beanstalk again. Up, up, up he went, and crossed the desert lands to the great doorway. For the second time the giant's wife opened the door.

'I shouldn't be letting you in,' she said. 'Last time you were here, a bag of gold went missing.'

'Did it indeed?' said Jack. Then the floor-boards began to shudder and the house shook to its foundations.

'Alas, alas, there is my husband come home!' said the giant's wife, and she hid Jack behind the woodpile. Again the loud footsteps stamped up to the door and the great voice roared:

'Fee fi fo fum,
I smell the blood of an Englishman.
Be he alive or be he dead,
I'll grind his bones to make my bread.'

'It is only the cows you put by for your supper,' the woman replied.

The giant grunted and sat down. He ate and ate until at last he leant back in his chair and called for his hen. A brown hen flew onto the table. 'Lay!' roared the giant, and the hen laid a golden egg. 'Lay!' roared the giant again, and the hen laid another golden egg, and another, and another, until the giant's head drooped and the kitchen began to echo with his snores.

Jack nipped out from behind the woodpile, snatched up the hen and ran out of the great house. The hen clucked in alarm and woke the giant, who picked up his club and lumbered after Jack. But Jack was past the desert lands, down the beanstalk and in through his bedroom window before the giant had gone more than a few paces.

For many months Jack and his mother lived in luxury, but eventually Jack grew bored and decided to climb the beanstalk one last time. Up, up, up he went, through the desert lands and on to the huge doorway. For the third time the giant's wife opened the door.

'You can't come in,' she said. 'My husband will skin you alive. Last time you came here, his magic hen disappeared.'

'Did it?' said Jack, pretending he knew nothing about the matter. But when the giant's wife turned to close the door, he slipped inside and hid in the washing bowl.

Almost immediately the floor-boards began to shudder and the walls began to shake, and a huge voice bellowed:

'Fee fi fo fum,
I smell the blood of an Englishman.
Be he alive or be he dead,
I'll grind his bones to make my bread.'

'It is only that sack of pigs you were saving for supper,' replied the giant's wife.

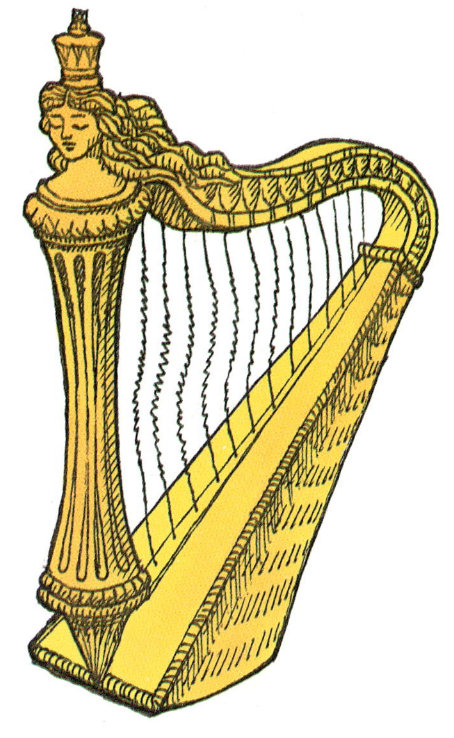

The giant grunted and sat down. He ate and ate until he leant back in his chair and called for his harp. His wife brought out a beautiful gold harp and laid it on the table.

'Play!' roared the giant. Immediately the strings of the harp began to play a beautiful melody.

The giant's head nodded. Even Jack felt drowsy. But when he was sure the giant was asleep, Jack nipped out of the washing bowl and snatched up the magic harp. No sooner had he touched it than the harp shouted, 'Master! Master!' and the giant woke up. Jack ran out of the great house, and the giant came after him.

He ran like the wind across the desert lands and the giant was close behind. He climbed down the beanstalk, which shook and swayed and shuddered as the giant followed.

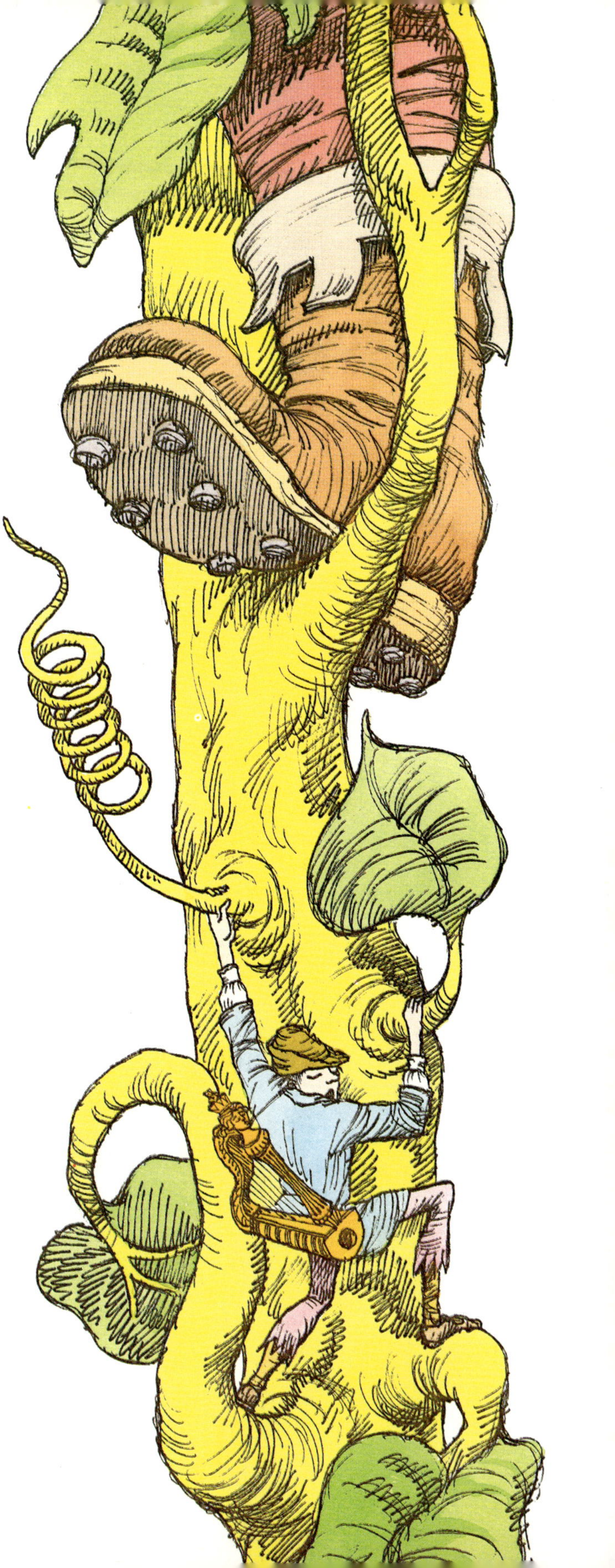

‘Quick! Quick! Fetch me an axe, Mother!’ cried Jack as he jumped into his bedroom. The giant was coming closer and closer. Jack rushed into the garden and started to chop down the beanstalk.

The beanstalk creaked, the giant roared, and with a tremendous crash all came tumbling down. The giant lay dead in the garden. Jack decided there and then to give up adventuring, and he and his mother lived in peace and plenty until the end of their days.

THE LITTLE RED HEN

There was once a little red hen who lived with a dog, a cat and a goose. One day the little red hen found a grain of wheat.

'Who will plant this wheat?' she asked.

'Not I,' said the dog.

'Not I,' said the cat.

'Not I,' said the goose.

'Then I'll plant it myself,' said the little red hen. And she did.

The wheat grew up green and tall. When summer came, the grains ripened in the sun and the wheat turned golden yellow. Now it was ready for cutting.

'Who will cut this wheat?' asked the little red hen.

'Not I,' said the dog.
'Not I,' said the cat.
'Not I,' said the goose.
'Then I'll cut it myself,' said the little red hen. And she did.

Now the wheat was ready for threshing, to get rid of the hard husks round each grain.

'Who will thresh this wheat?' asked the little red hen.

'Not I,' said the dog.
'Not I,' said the cat.
'Not I,' said the goose.
'Then I'll thresh it myself,' said the little red hen. And she did.

Now the grains of wheat were ready for milling, to grind them into flour.

'Who will take this wheat to the mill?' asked the little red hen.

'Not I,' said the dog.
'Not I,' said the cat.
'Not I,' said the goose.
'Then I'll take it myself,'

said the little red hen. And she did.

The miller ground the corn into flour, ready for baking. 'Who will bake this flour into bread?' asked the little red hen.

'Not I,' said the dog.

'Not I,' said the cat.

'Not I,' said the goose.

'Then I'll bake it myself,' said the little red hen. And she did.

When the bread came out of the oven all brown and crusty, the little red hen set it down on the table.

'Who will eat this bread?' she asked.

'I will!' said the dog.

'I will!' said the cat.

'I will!' said the goose.

'No, you won't!' said the little red hen. 'I'll eat it myself!' And she did, down to the very last crumb.

THE ELVES AND THE SHOEMAKER

There was once a shoemaker who was so poor he had only enough leather to make one pair of shoes.

Late one night he cut the precious leather and carefully laid the pieces on his workbench, ready for sewing the following day. But when he came down the next morning, an amazing sight met his eyes. In place of the little pile of leather pieces lay the finest pair of shoes he had ever seen. So small were the stitches and so skilful the work that the shoes sold for twice as much as the shoemaker expected. Now he had money enough to buy leather for two pairs of shoes.

Once again the shoemaker cut out the leather and laid the pieces on his bench before he went to bed. This time there were two pairs of shoes when he came down in the morning. The shoemaker looked at the tiny stitches and neat little holes in the leather. 'This is the work of a master craftsman,' he said to his wife. The shoes sold for twice the price he expected, and now the shoemaker could buy leather enough for four pairs of shoes.

Time went by and the shoemaker grew rich. People came from far and wide to buy his beautiful shoes. He had only to lay out the pieces of leather at night for the shoes to be completed by morning. But the shoemaker's wife was consumed with curiosity. She wanted to know who it was that came in the night and hammered and pierced and stitched so skilfully. So she persuaded her husband to sit up and watch with her one night.

Not long after the candles had been snuffed, when all was quiet, two tiny men in rags and

tatters appeared from under the floor. They climbed onto the bench, and all night long they hammered and pierced and stitched. They sang as they worked and their fingers flew so fast the shoemaker could hardly believe his eyes.

By first light forty pairs of shoes lay on the bench. The shoemaker stood up, but the little men disappeared through a crack in the floor-boards before he could say a word.

'How can we thank them? What can we give these master cobblers?' he asked his wife, who was quick with an answer.

'Clothes, Husband, clothes. Did you not see they were dressed in rags and tatters? Why, I can sew them a suit of clothes, and you can make them a pair of boots.'

When the little men appeared the following night, there were no pieces of leather for them to hammer, pierce and stitch. Instead two piles of tiny garments lay on the bench –

two little hats, one with a feather, two tunics with embroidered belts, two pairs of tiny woven tights and two pairs of fancy leather boots. The elves, for elves they were, put on their new clothes and capered about, laughing with glee and singing:

'Fine boys now must find the door,
Cobbling we shall do no more!'

They rushed about the room, and when at last they found the door, they lifted the latch and skipped out into the night, still laughing and singing. The shoemaker and his wife never saw the elves again, but they continued to prosper, and good luck stayed with them to the end of their days.

THE PRINCESS AND THE PEA

Once upon a time there was a prince who longed to marry a real princess. He travelled the world, but he could never find a princess who was just right. One was too tall, another too small; one was too pretty, another too plain; one was too quiet, another too talkative. There was always something wrong. Not one of them seemed quite like a *real* princess.

Then one night a dreadful storm broke over the prince's castle. Thunder roared, lightning flashed, and rain poured down in torrents. The king heard someone knocking at the castle door and went to see who it was. There, standing in the rain, was a girl who said she was a princess. Rain streamed down her hair and face. She certainly didn't look like a real princess.

'We shall soon find out,' said the queen, and she went into the bedroom kept for visitors. She pulled off all the bedclothes and placed a small dried pea on the bedstead. Upon this she piled twenty fat mattresses and twenty-five plump quilts. Then she put the princess to bed.

'And how did you sleep, my dear?' asked the queen the next morning.

'Wretchedly, I'm afraid,' said the princess. 'I hardly slept at all. I don't know what was in my bed, but it was certainly something terribly hard. I'm black and blue all over.'

The queen smiled. The king smiled. The prince jumped up and clapped his hands. Here was a *real* princess at last. She had felt the pea through twenty fat mattresses and twenty-five plump quilts. Only a real princess could have been so sensitive.

The prince and the princess were married and the pea was put on show in the royal museum. If it hasn't been stolen, it stands there still.

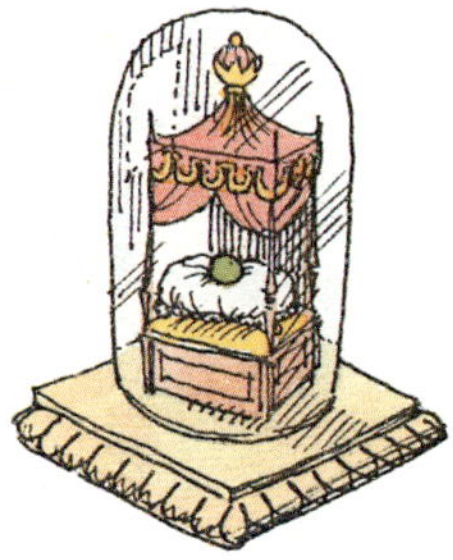